CLASSICAL COMPOSERS

# *Johannes* BRAHMS

by Joanne Mattern
with Consultation by John Viscardi,
Executive Director of Classic Lyric Arts
illustrated by Marilena Perilli

Egremont, Massachusetts

**Classical Composers** has been produced and published by Red Chair Press Books for Young Readers:
Red Chair Press LLC PO Box 333 South Egremont, MA 01258
www.redchairpress.com

 Download a Free Activity Guide on our website.

For more information about Classic Lyric Arts, visit www.classiclyricarts.org.

Names: Mattern, Joanne, 1963- author. | Viscardi, John, consultant. | Perilli, Marilena, illustrator.

Title: Johannes Brahms / by Joanne Mattern, with consultation by John Viscardi, executive director of Classic Lyric Arts ; illustrated by Marilena Perilli.

Description: Egremont, Massachusetts : Red Chair Press, [2026] | Series: Mattern, Joanne, 1963- Classical composers. | Interest age level: 008-012. | Includes bibliographical references and index. | Summary: Johannes Brahms (1833–1897) was a German Romantic-era composer known for emotional depth and classical structure. He wrote symphonies, piano works, and choral music, blending tradition with innovation to become one of history's great composers.--Publisher.

Identifiers: LCCN: 2025939691 | ISBN: 9781967893003 (library hardcover) | 9781967893010 (paperback) | 9781967893034 (S&L ePub 3) | 9781967893027 (S&L ebook PDF) | 9781967893058 (audiobook)

Subjects: LCSH: Brahms, Johannes, 1833-1897--Juvenile literature. | Composers--Germany--Biography--Juvenile literature. | CYAC: Brahms, Johannes, 1833-1897. | Composers--Germany--Biography. | LCGFT: Biographies. | BISAC: JUVENILE NONFICTION / Music / Classical. | JUVENILE NONFICTION / Biography & Autobiography / Music. | JUVENILE NONFICTION / Biography & Autobiography / Performing Arts.

Classification: LCC: ML410.B8 M38 2026 | DDC: 780.92--dc23



**Image credits:** 4 Bridgeman Images; 14 Bridgeman Images; 21 Lebrecht Music & Art/Alamy; 22 Chronicle/Alamy; 24 Lebrecht Music & Art/Alamy; 26 Fritz Luckhardt (1843-1894)/Courtesy of the Wien Museum; 28 Archivio GBB/Alamy; 31 Panther Media Global/Alamy

**Illustrations:** Marilena Perilli, except p. 7 by Joe LeMonnier

Printed in the United States of America

0426 1P F26CG

# Table of Contents

# A Musical Home

Johannes Brahms was one of the most famous **composers** of all time. He wrote music 200 years ago that people love to hear and perform today. Brahms lived at a time when people had different ideas about what classical music should sound like. Brahms used these ideas to create many different kinds of music.

Johannes Brahms was born in Hamburg, Germany, on May 7, 1833. He had an older sister and a younger brother. Johannes' father was a musician. He played the double bass and the French horn in a musical group called the Hamburg **Philharmonic** Society.

Johannes' family did not have a lot of money. But they did have music. Johannes grew up listening to his father play. Soon, he wanted to learn music too.

B#

**B SHARP:** Johannes and his sister were close, but he did not get along with his younger brother, Fritz. Once he wrote a letter to his father saying he would not stay at the family house because Fritz was there.

Sweden
North Sea
Baltic Sea
Denmark
Netherlands
Hamburg
United Kingdom
North German Confederation
London
Belg.
Paris
Bavaria
Vienna
Austria-Hungary
French Empire
Switz.
Italy
Ottoman Empire
Serbia
Rome
Papal States
Spain
Mediterranean Sea
Greece

Johannes told his father he wanted to learn to play music. His father could play almost every classical instrument. He offered to teach Johannes the violin or the cello. Johannes said no. He wanted to play the piano. His father agreed to this choice. He found a teacher named Otto F.W. Cossel to teach Johannes.

Johannes started taking piano lessons when he was just seven years old. Cossel was a good teacher. But after a few years, he had taught Johannes everything he knew. He sent Johannes to another teacher named Eduard Marxsen. Marxsen was a well-known Hamburg piano teacher. He loved working with Johannes.

Unlike many music students, Johannes loved to practice. He would often stay up very late in the evenings to play the piano.

B#

**B SHARP:** Johannes started composing music when he was eleven years old.

B#

**B SHARP:** Johannes often brought books to read between his times playing piano at bars.

Brahms' family was still very poor. The young man needed to earn money. So, Johannes started playing dance music. He played in bars, inns, and dance halls all over Hamburg. Many of these places were not very nice especially for a young teenager. Johannes didn't care. He enjoyed playing piano anywhere he was.

# Brahms on Tour

In 1850, Brahms met a famous violinist named Eduard Reményi. Reményi and Brahms went on **tour**. They played music all over Germany.

Traveling helped Brahms learn more about music. He heard regional folk songs. Later he would use folk **melodies** in his own work.

Brahms also met many famous musicians. The most famous was Franz Liszt. Liszt played a style of music called romantic. He was very dramatic. Liszt even broke pianos with his wild and energetic playing!

Even though the period of about 1789 until 1837 is called the Romantic Era, the music was not what we think of as traditionally romantic today. It was wild and emotional and filled with drama.

B# **B SHARP:** Brahms did not like Liszt or his friends. Even though Liszt could help Brahms' career, the young pianist did not have much to do with him.

When he was 20 years old, Brahms met Robert and Clara Schumann. They were both famous composers. Robert loved the way Brahms played. He even wrote an article about Brahms for a music magazine. After this, people began paying more attention to the young composer.

But Brahms was embarrassed about what Schumann wrote. He worried that he would not be as good as people thought he should be.

Robert Schumann

Clara Schumann

Robert and Clara Schumann were great friends to Brahms. Then, in 1854, Robert died. Brahms traveled to Vienna, Austria, to stay with Clara. He helped take care of her children. Brahms and Clara would be great friends for the rest of his life. Some people think Brahms fell in love with Clara. In 1863, he would move to Vienna.

Brahms moved to this home in Vienna, Austria when he was 30 years old and he lived here until he died 34 years later.

# Different Styles

During this time, there was a big argument about what music should sound like. Some composers liked the classical style. Classical music was pretty and calm. Other people liked Romantic music. Romantic music was loud and dramatic. It was filled with drama and surprises. Some composers wrote music based on stories or poems.

Brahms liked both kinds of music. He combined both styles in his own work. Brahms' music had power and emotion. But it was also pretty and full of melody.

# Brahms' Greatest Works 

1868 was a big year for Brahms. He wrote a **lullaby** called "Wiegenlied." Today it is known as "Brahms' Lullaby." Almost everyone has heard this beautiful song.

In 1868, Brahms also wrote a piece called *A German* ***Requiem***. Brahms wrote the piece for his mother, who had died in 1865. Brahms filled the requiem with love and calm sounds. His music made people cry.

# Brahms and Beethoven

Many composers write lots of **symphonies**. But Brahms only wrote four. It took him 21 years to write his first symphony. He did not finish it until 1876, at age 44.

Brahms was nervous about writing a symphony. He was afraid he would be compared to Ludwig van Beethoven. Beethoven's symphonies were famous and popular at the time. But audiences really liked Brahms' symphonies too!

B#

**B SHARP:** Unlike many composers, Brahms never wrote an **opera**.

# Later Years

Brahms wrote lots of music after he moved to Vienna in 1863. But in 1890, he said he was **retiring** from music. Brahms' retirement did not last long. He went on to write a lot more music after that.

Brahms enjoyed going to concerts and parks in Vienna. He took long walks in the woods. Brahms never got married. But he had lots of friends and enjoyed spending time with them.

Brahms continued to write music in the 1890s. He also toured Europe. He performed and **conducted** music in many different countries.

Johannes Brahms died of cancer on April 3, 1897. He was 63 years old. He is buried in his favorite city, Vienna. More than 100 years later, people all over the world still love and perform his work.

Bach Beethoven Brahms

**B# B SHARP:** Johann Sebastian Bach, Ludwig van Beethoven, and Johannes Brahms are known as the "Three Bs" of classical music.

# Important Dates in Johannes Brahms' Life

**1833** Johannes Brahms is born in Hamburg, Germany.

**1840** Brahms begins taking piano lessons.

**1850** Brahms tours Germany with violinist Eduard Reményi.

**1853** Brahms meets Robert and Clara Schumann.

**1863** Brahms moves to Vienna, Austria.

**1868** Brahms writes his "Lullaby" and *A German Requiem.*

**1876** Brahms finishes his first symphony.

**1890** Brahms retires but continues to compose and perform.

**1897** Brahms dies in Vienna on April 3.

Brahms' grave in Vienna, with a marble carving of his face. To the left of Brahms' grave is that of composer Johann Strauss II, a close friend.

# Glossary

**composers** people who write music

**conducted** led an orchestra or chorus

**lullaby** a soft, quiet song often played or sung to help a child fall asleep

**melodies** series of notes that make up a tune

**opera** a story set to music for one or more singers and an orchestra

**philharmonic** devoted to orchestra music

**requiem** a musical composition for the dead

**retiring** no longer working

**symphonies** long pieces of music for an orchestra

**tour** a journey in which several places are visited and (in music) where performances are held in different cities

# Read More About Brahms

**Venezia, Mike**. *Johannes Brahms (Getting to Know the World's Greatest Composers* series). Children's Press, 1999.

**Rachlin, Ann**. *Brahms (Famous Children* series). B.E.S. Publishing, 1993.

# Index